WOMEN'S *Anxiety & Stress* DEVOTIONAL

90-Day, 5-Minute
Christian Devotional for Women to
Find Peace, Calm Overthinking, and
Trust God in Difficult Moments

ANCHORED GRACE
PUBLISHING

A Gift for You

Thank you for choosing this devotional.

To support your journey of faith, we created a special gift bundle for our readers.

Inside the Anchored Grace Reader Gift Bundle, you will receive:

- A free digital devotional
- Printable prayer journal pages
- Scripture reflection cards
- Bonus devotionals for different seasons of life
- Daily encouragement from Anchored Grace

Simply scan the QR code below or visit the link to receive your free bundle.

devo.anchoredgraces.com/anxietygift

Scan the QR code with your phone camera or type the link into your browser.

We pray these resources continue to encourage your heart each day.

Finding Peace
in God's Presence

"My soul finds rest in God alone; my salvation comes from him. Truly he is my rock and my salvation; he is my fortress, I will never be shaken."

Psalm 62:1-2

DEVOTION

Remember, dear one, in the busyness of daily life, finding peace begins by cultivating intentional moments in God's presence, where you can truly be yourself and experience His loving embrace.

REFLECTION

What does it mean for you to find peace in God's presence today? Can you identify a moment when you felt His calming influence in your life?

____

____

____

____

PRAYER

Dear Lord, I come before You seeking the peace that only You can provide. Help me to pause, breathe, and embrace Your presence in every moment of my day. Amen.

In His presence, worries dissolve, and peace finds a home.

Be Still and Know

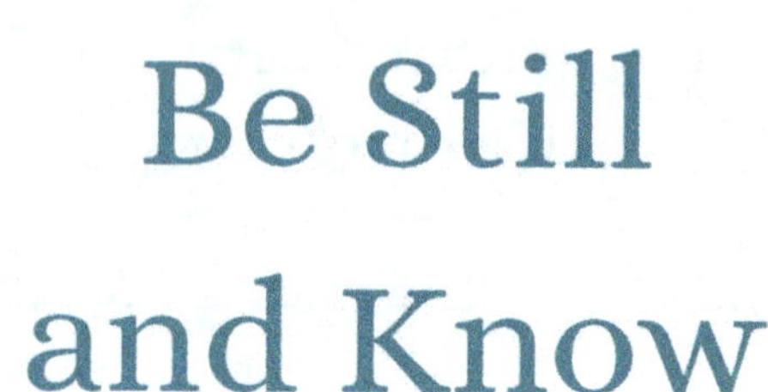

"Be still and know that I am God."

Psalm 46:10

DEVOTION

When overwhelmed, take time to acknowledge that in the stillness, you can find clarity and strength for your journey ahead.

REFLECTION

What does it mean for you to be still in the midst of your busy life? How can you create moments of quiet to truly know and feel God's presence?

____

____

____

____

PRAYER

Dear God, help me to find peace in the chaos of my days. Grant me the wisdom to pause, reflect, and connect with You, even for just a moment. Thank You for Your constant presence in my life.

In the stillness, we discover the richness of God's love.

Stillness in God's Presence

"Yes, my soul, find rest in God; my hope comes from him. Truly he is my rock and my salvation; he is my fortress, I will not be shaken."

Psalm 62:5-6

DEVOTION

Embracing moments of stillness can transform our chaotic lives into encounters with peace, reminding us that God is always with us, ready to offer His presence as our refuge.

REFLECTION

What does it feel like for you to truly stop and rest in God's presence amid the busyness of life?

____

____

____

____

PRAYER

Dear God, help me to find peace and stillness in my heart. Guide me to recognize Your presence throughout my day and to draw strength from that quiet connection.

In the stillness, I hear God's whispers of love and direction.

A Quiet Heart in a Noisy World

"In repentance and rest is your salvation, in quietness and trust is your strength."

Isaiah 30:15

DEVOTION

In the whirlwind of being a woman and daily responsibilities, remember to carve out moments of quiet for your soul, finding strength and peace amidst the noise.

REFLECTION

What are the noisy distractions in your life that keep you from experiencing the peace and stillness you crave? How might you set aside time today to cultivate a quieter heart amidst the busyness of womanhood and daily responsibilities?

____

____

____

____

PRAYER

Dear Lord, help me find moments of stillness in the chaos. Grant me a quiet heart that rests in Your presence, and let me be mindful of Your peace in my everyday life.

Peace is not the absence of noise, but the presence of Christ in our hearts.

The Gift of
Quiet Moments

"Come to me, all you who are weary and burdened, and I will give you rest."

Matthew 11:28-30

DEVOTION

Embrace the gift of quiet moments; they are where your heart can find peace and your spirit can be rejuvenated.

REFLECTION

What does it feel like for you to carve out those quiet moments in your day? How can you intentionally embrace stillness amid the busy rhythms of life?

____

____

____

____

PRAYER

Dear God, thank you for the gift of quiet moments amidst our busy lives. Help me to recognize and savor these times, knowing they are precious treasures that draw me closer to You.

In the stillness, we often hear the whispers of our hearts.

Listening for God's Whisper

"And your ears shall hear a word behind you, saying, 'This is the way, walk in it,' whenever you turn to the right or to the left."

Isaiah 30:21

DEVOTION

In the still moments of your day, remember that cultivating space for God's whispers can lead you toward renewed purpose and serenity.

REFLECTION

What distractions in your life might be keeping you from truly hearing God's whisper? How can you create moments of quiet to listen more closely?

____

____

____

____

PRAYER

Dear God, help me to quiet my heart and mind so that I can hear Your gentle whispers. Guide me in moments of stillness, and open my ears to Your loving voice.

In the stillness, God's whispers become clearer, leading us gently along the path of life.

One Week Together

You've just completed your first week of devotionals.

If these reflections have brought peace or encouragement into your day, would you consider sharing a short Amazon review?

https://devo.anchoredgraces.com/anxiety

Your words help other women discover devotionals that may support them on their own faith journey.

Thank you for spending these moments in reflection.

The Gentle Voice of God

"In the stillness, you will hear His whisper, guiding you through the complexities of life."

1 Kings 19:12

DEVOTION

Trust that in the busyness of life, God's voice is often soft, calling you back to moments of peace and clarity.

REFLECTION

What whispers of comfort or guidance is God gently sharing with you today, amidst the noise of your busy life? Can you pause for a moment to hear Him?

____

____

____

____

PRAYER

Dear God, thank you for your gentle voice that calms our hearts and directs our paths. Help me to slow down and intentionally listen for Your guidance in my daily life.

In the stillness of the heart, we often find God's softest whisper.

The Voice That Calms

He replied, "You of little faith, why are you so afraid?" Then he got up and rebuked the winds and the waves, and it was completely calm.

Matthew 8:26

DEVOTION

When life feels tumultuous, remember to pause and listen for that still, comforting voice that brings calm to the chaos.

REFLECTION

What voices do you allow to speak into your life, and how do they influence your peace and well-being?

____

____

____

____

PRAYER

Dear God, thank You for always being a calming presence in our lives. Help me to recognize and lean into Your voice amidst the chaos of daily life. Amen.

The quiet whisper of His love can calm the loudest storms within.

Peace That Passes Understanding

Philippians 4:7 reminds us that the peace of God, which transcends all understanding, will guard our hearts and minds in Christ Jesus. Embrace this divine tranquility as you navigate the beautiful yet tumultuous journey of womanhood and life.

DEVOTION

True peace comes when we release our burdens to God, knowing He is in control of every situation we face.

REFLECTION

What are the situations in your life that challenge your peace, and how can you invite God into those moments today?

____

____

____

____

PRAYER

Dear Lord, help me to find rest in Your presence and trust that You are in control. Fill my heart with Your peace that transcends all understanding, today and every day.

Peace is not the absence of trouble, but the assurance of His presence.

Peace That Transcends

"Peace I leave with you; my peace I give you. I do not give to you as the world gives. Do not let your hearts be troubled and do not be afraid."

John 14:27

DEVOTION

Embrace the moments of stillness amidst your busyness—it's in those spaces where God's transcendent peace can refresh your spirit.

REFLECTION

What weighs on your heart that keeps you from experiencing the peace you long for? Can you identify moments when you've felt a peace that transcended your circumstances? How can you invite that peace into your life today?

____

____

____

____

PRAYER

Dear God, help me find your peace that surpasses all understanding. May I feel your presence in every moment, calming my heart and guiding my thoughts. Amen.

True peace is not the absence of chaos but the presence of God.

Anxious for Nothing

Matthew 6:34 reminds us to "not worry about tomorrow, for tomorrow will worry about itself."

DEVOTION

In each moment of worry, there is an invitation to embrace the present and let go of what we cannot control.

REFLECTION

What worries or anxieties are you holding onto today, and how might you lay them down at Jesus' feet?

____

____

____

____

PRAYER

Dear God, as I navigate the worries of life, help me to trust in Your presence and peace. Remind me that I can release my fears into Your caring hands today.

Anxiety loses its power when surrendered to the One who holds our tomorrows.

Casting
Your Cares

"Cast all your anxiety on Him because
He cares for you."

1 Peter 5:7

DEVOTION

Even in the busiest seasons of life,
remember that His presence brings
solace; you are never alone in your
journey.

REFLECTION

What moments in your life remind you that you are never alone, even amid challenges and joy?

____

____

____

____

PRAYER

Dear Lord, thank you for your constant presence in my life. Help me to recognize your love in every moment, guiding me with peace and assurance.

His presence is the gentle whisper in the chaos of womanhood.

He Carries Your Burdens

"Cast all your anxiety on him because he cares for you."

1 Peter 5:7

DEVOTION

Life teaches us that sharing our worries with God can bring profound relief, reminding us that we do not have to navigate our challenges alone.

REFLECTION

What burdens are you carrying today that you need to lay down at His feet?

____

____

____

____

PRAYER

Dear Lord, thank you for being our source of strength. Help me to trust in You as I cast my cares upon You, knowing You are always here to carry my burdens.

Let Him lighten your load, for He is always ready to lift you up.

God
Is Your Refuge

"I will say of the Lord, 'He is my refuge and my fortress, my God, in whom I trust.'"

Psalm 91:2

DEVOTION

Remember, dear one, that God is not just a destination for your burdens; He is your safe haven and steady stronghold amidst life's storms.

REFLECTION

What does it mean for you, in your daily life as a mother and woman, to find refuge in God amidst your challenges and responsibilities?

____

____

____

____

PRAYER

Dear Lord, thank You for being my safe haven and strength. Help me to lean on You when life feels overwhelming, and remind me that I am never alone in this journey.

Finding sanctuary in Him transforms the noise of our lives into a melody of peace.

The Lord Is Your Shepherd

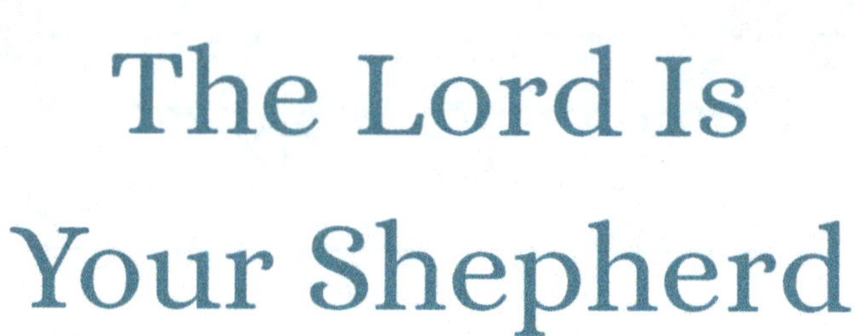

"The Lord is my shepherd; I shall not want. He makes me lie down in green pastures. He leads me beside still waters. He restores my soul."

Psalm 23:1-3

DEVOTION

In the embrace of His care, trust that it's okay to step back and refuel, for the Lord watches over your heart and provides the peace your spirit longs for.

REFLECTION

What does it mean for you to trust that the Lord is guiding you, especially in the midst of your daily responsibilities as a mother and a woman of faith?

____

____

____

____

PRAYER

Dear Lord, thank You for being our Shepherd, guiding us with Your loving care. Help us to lean on You in times of uncertainty and to trust in Your path for our lives.

Even in the busyness of life, His guidance is always available to those who seek it.

Comforted by God's Nearness

"The LORD is close to the brokenhearted and saves those who are crushed in spirit."

Psalm 34:18

DEVOTION

God's nearness is a constant source of strength, reminding us that even in our most challenging moments, we are never truly alone.

REFLECTION

What does it mean for you to feel God's presence in your everyday life, especially during moments of challenge or joy? Can you recall a time when you sensed His nearness?

____

____

____

____

PRAYER

Dear Lord, thank You for being ever-present in my life. Help me to recognize Your comfort and embrace Your love amidst the busyness of life and daily responsibilities.

God's nearness transforms our trials into testimonies of grace.

Peace in the Midst of Change

"Be still, and know that I am God."

Psalm 46:10

DEVOTION

In the midst of change, remember that God's peace is a constant, waiting for you to embrace it.

REFLECTION

What change are you currently facing in your life, and how can you invite God's peace into that situation?

____

____

____

____

PRAYER

Dear Lord, thank you for being a constant source of peace in our lives, even when everything around us feels uncertain. Help me to trust in Your plans and to lean on Your strength as I navigate through these changes.

True peace is not the absence of change but the presence of faith.

Choosing Peace in Uncertainty

"You will keep in perfect peace those whose minds are steadfast because they trust in you."

Isaiah 26:3

DEVOTION

Choose to embrace the peace that comes from trusting that you are not alone in your journey through uncertainty.

REFLECTION

What areas of your life feel uncertain right now, and how might choosing peace in those spaces transform your experience?

____

____

____

____

PRAYER

Dear God, in the midst of uncertainty, help me to find my anchor in You. Grant me the wisdom to choose peace over worry and to trust in Your guiding hand. Amen.

Peace is not the absence of chaos, but the presence of tranquility in the midst of it.

Peace When You Don't Understand

"You will keep in perfect peace those whose minds are steadfast, because they trust in you."

Isaiah 26:3

DEVOTION

Even when circumstances feel beyond our understanding, we can find peace by trusting in God's perfect plan for our lives and our families.

REFLECTION

What situations in your life currently feel overwhelming or confusing, and how might you seek peace in those moments of uncertainty?

____

____

____

____

PRAYER

Dear Lord, grant me the peace that surpasses understanding as I navigate the complexities of life. Help me to trust in Your divine plan, even when I can't see the way forward.

In the midst of chaos, the heart can find a quiet place of refuge.

Finding Peace in the Unknown

"And after you have suffered a little while, the God of all grace, who has called you to his eternal glory in Christ, will himself restore, confirm, strengthen, and establish you."

1 Peter 5:10

DEVOTION

There is peace for every anxious heart in surrendering your worries to God, trusting that He is guiding you through all the uncertainties and unknowns you face as a woman.

REFLECTION

What unknown situations in your life as a woman are causing you worry or anxiety right now? How might you invite God's peace into these moments by surrendering your fears and trusting in His greater plan?

____

____

____

____

PRAYER

Dear God, thank You for Your constant presence when anxiety and uncertainty fill my heart. Help me find true peace as I navigate the unknowns of my journey, and remind me that You are always guiding, restoring, and strengthening me.

In the silence of uncertainty, an anxious heart can find peace in God's gentle presence.

Letting Go of Control

"For I know the plans I have for you," declares the Lord, "plans to prosper you and not to harm you, plans to give you hope and a future."

Jeremiah 29:11

DEVOTION

Letting go of control frees us to experience the joy and beauty of life's unexpected moments.

REFLECTION

What does letting go of control look like in your daily life, and how can you embrace the beauty of uncertainty as you navigate the present and beyond?

____

____

____

____

PRAYER

Dear God, help me to release my grip on the things I cannot control. Grant me peace in knowing that You hold my life and my loved ones in Your hands. Thank You for guiding me as I learn to trust in Your plans.

Trusting in God's timing is the first step toward freedom from the burdens of control.

Three Weeks of Reflection

You've now spent several weeks walking through these devotionals.

If this book has encouraged your heart, a brief Amazon review helps other women find the same encouragement.

https://devo.anchoredgraces.com/anxiety

Your experience may guide someone else toward the hope they are searching for.

Thank you for being here.

The Strength of Surrender

"This is what the Sovereign Lord, the Holy One of Israel, says: 'In repentance and rest is your salvation, in quietness and trust is your strength.'"

Isaiah 30:15

DEVOTION

Sometimes, the greatest strength comes from letting go and allowing God's grace to guide us.

REFLECTION

What does surrender mean for you in this season of your life, and how might embracing it lead to newfound strength and peace?

____

____

____

____

PRAYER

Dear God, help me to release my burdens and trust in Your plan. Grant me the courage to surrender my worries and find strength in Your presence every day.

True strength is found not in holding on tightly, but in the quiet power of letting go.

Finding Rest in Surrender

Romans 12:1-2 reminds us, "Therefore, I urge you, sisters, in view of God's mercy, to offer your bodies as living sacrifices, holy and pleasing to God—this is your true and proper worship. Do not conform to the pattern of this world, but be transformed by the renewing of your mind."

DEVOTION

When you surrender your worries to God, you create a pathway for peace to flow into your life.

REFLECTION

What does surrendering to God in your daily life look like, and how can you embrace it as a source of rest amidst your responsibilities?

____

____

____

____

PRAYER

Dear God, help me to release my burdens into Your hands. Grant me the peace that comes from trusting You fully and enable me to find solace in surrender.

Surrender is not giving up; it's opening your heart to a greater plan.

The Peace of Letting Go

"Therefore do not worry about tomorrow, for tomorrow will worry about itself. Each day has enough trouble of its own."

Matthew 6:34

DEVOTION

Sometimes, the greatest peace comes from the courage to release what we cannot control.

REFLECTION

What burdens are you carrying that you need to let go of in order to embrace the peace God offers you?

____

____

____

____

PRAYER

Lord, grant me the courage to release my worries and trust in Your plan. Help me to embrace the serenity that comes with surrendering my burdens to You, knowing that Your guidance is always with me.

True peace comes when we release the need to control and allow God to lead.

Courage to Let Go

"Forget the former things; do not dwell on the past. See, I am doing a new thing! Now it springs up; do you not perceive it?"

Isaiah 43:18-19

DEVOTION

Letting go can be a profound act of courage that opens you to the joys and opportunities awaiting you in this new season of life.

REFLECTION

What are the things in your life that you hold onto tightly, and how might offering them to God bring you peace and new opportunities?

____

____

____

____

PRAYER

Dear Lord, help me to find the courage to release what no longer serves me. Teach me to trust in Your plan and embrace the freedom that comes from letting go.

Letting go is not losing; it's making space for what truly matters.

Living with Open Hands

"Open your mouth wide, and I will fill it, says the Lord."

Psalm 81:10

DEVOTION

In this season of life, filled with various responsibilities and roles, remember that openness invites blessings. When we release our tight grip on control and expectations, we allow God to fill us with joy, peace, and unexpected moments of beauty.

REFLECTION

What does it mean for you to live with open hands, inviting both gifting and letting go in your daily life? How might this practice transform your relationship with your family and your own sense of purpose?

____

____

____

____

PRAYER

Lord, help me to embrace life with open hands. Teach me to receive your blessings gratefully and to release my worries and fears into your care. May I find joy in the gift of each moment.

Living with open hands unlocks the blessings of both giving and receiving.

Letting God Carry the Load

"Rejoice in the Lord and let your gentleness be evident to all. The Lord is near. Do not be anxious about anything, but in every situation, by prayer and petition, with thanksgiving, present your requests to God."

Philippians 4:4-6

DEVOTION

Letting God carry the load means allowing yourself the freedom to lean on His strength when life feels too heavy.

REFLECTION

What burdens are you carrying today that you could hand over to God? How might your life change if you let Him take the weight of those worries?

____

____

____

____

PRAYER

Dear God, please help me to trust You with my burdens. Teach me to release my worries into Your capable hands, knowing that You care for me deeply. May I feel Your peace enveloping me as I let go.

Sometimes the strongest thing we can do is to simply let go and let God.

Trusting God's Bigger Picture

"And my God will meet all your needs according to the riches of his glory in Christ Jesus."

Philippians 4:19

DEVOTION

You may not see the bigger picture today, but trust that God is crafting something magnificent beyond your understanding.

REFLECTION

What are some areas in your life where you're struggling to trust in God's bigger picture, and how can you take a step towards surrendering that burden to Him?

____

____

____

____

PRAYER

Dear Lord, help me to see beyond my immediate worries and to trust in Your perfect plan. Give me the strength to lean into Your guidance and the peace that comes from knowing You're always working for my good.

Faith is not believing that God will do what you ask, but trusting that He will do what is best.

He Sees the Whole Picture

"I lift my eyes to the hills—where does my help come from? My help comes from the Lord, the Maker of heaven and earth."

Psalm 121:1-2

DEVOTION

Trust that even when we feel lost in the details, He is weaving a tapestry of grace that holds our entire journey in His capable hands.

REFLECTION

What areas of your life feel overwhelming right now, and how might trusting in God's vision help you navigate them?

____

____

____

____

PRAYER

Dear Lord, thank You for being the ultimate Author of our lives. Help me to see beyond today's trials and trust that You are orchestrating every detail for my good.

God sees the whole picture, even when our view is limited to just the frame.

He Works All Things for Good

Romans 8:28 reminds us that "in all things God works for the good of those who love him, who have been called according to his purpose."

DEVOTION

The comforting truth is that even when life feels chaotic and plans unravel, God uses every experience to shape us—and those we love—into something beautiful.

REFLECTION

What are the difficult situations in your life that you can surrender to God, trusting that He is weaving them into your story for a greater purpose? How can you remind yourself of His faithfulness in these moments?

____

____

____

____

PRAYER

Dear Lord, thank You for Your promise that You work all things for good. Help me to trust in Your plan, even when I can't see it, and to find peace in knowing that You hold my life in Your hands.

Every thread of our lives is woven with purpose, creating a beautiful tapestry only God can see.

You Are Not Alone

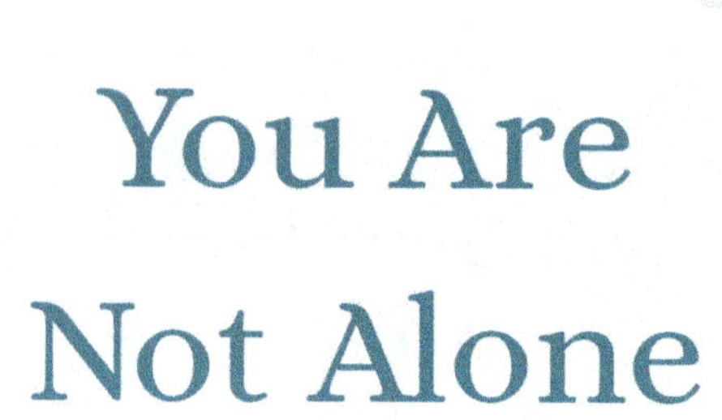

"Where can I go from your Spirit? Where can I flee from your presence? If I go up to the heavens, you are there; if I make my bed in the depths, you are there."

Psalm 139:7-10

DEVOTION

You are never alone; there are hearts around you that understand and share in your journey.

REFLECTION

What are the moments in your life when you've felt the strongest sense of solitude, and how has God's presence comforted you during these times?

____

____

____

____

PRAYER

Dear God, thank you for always being by my side, even during the hardest days. Help me to feel your presence and embrace the truth that I am never truly alone.

In the tapestry of life, the threads of solitude are woven with the presence of God's unwavering love.

You Are
Never Alone

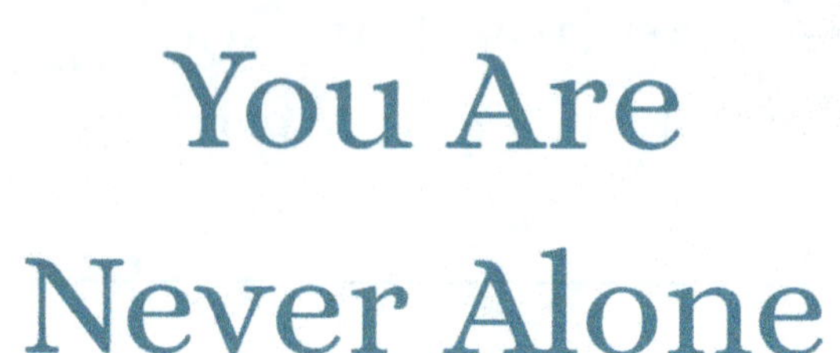

"The Lord himself goes before you and will be with you; he will never leave you nor forsake you. Do not be afraid; do not be discouraged."

Deuteronomy 31:8

DEVOTION

Remember, dear friend, even in your busiest or loneliest moments, you are never truly alone; God is always there, cheering you on and loving you deeply.

REFLECTION

What moment in your day feels the loneliest, and how can you invite God into that space to remind you of His presence?

____

____

____

____

PRAYER

Dear God, thank you for always being with us, especially in moments of solitude. Help us to feel your love and guidance as we navigate the complexities of life. Amen.

In every heartbeat, remember: You are cradled in love, surrounded by the unseen hand that holds your heart.

You Are Held

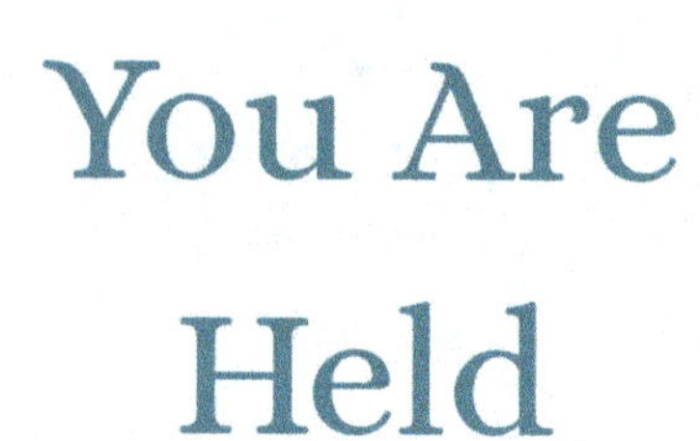

"Come to me, all you who are weary and burdened, and I will give you rest. Take my yoke upon you and learn from me, for I am gentle and humble in heart, and you will find rest for your souls."

Matthew 11:28-29

DEVOTION

You have the strength to face the challenges of womanhood, knowing that you are tenderly held and supported in all aspects of your life.

REFLECTION

What areas in your life do you feel burdened or uncertain right now, and how might recognizing that you're held in God's embrace change your perspective?

____

____

____

____

PRAYER

Dear Lord, thank you for the reminder that we are held in Your loving embrace. Help us to find comfort and strength in Your presence today as we navigate the challenges of life.

You are held, cherished beyond measure, and grounded in love.

The God Who Who Sees You

Genesis 16:13 tells us that Hagar, a woman in distress, encountered God in her loneliness. She gave this name to the Lord who spoke to her: "You are the God who sees me."

DEVOTION

The take-home message here is that God recognizes the unseen struggles of our hearts and reassures us that we are never truly invisible to Him.

REFLECTION

What moments in your life have made you feel invisible or overlooked? How can you lean into the truth that God sees you, even in the mundane or challenging seasons of life?

____

____

____

____

PRAYER

Dear God, thank You for being present in our lives and for seeing us even when we feel unseen. Help us to grasp the depth of Your love and awareness in our daily struggles and joys.

You are loved and seen by the One who knows you inside and out.

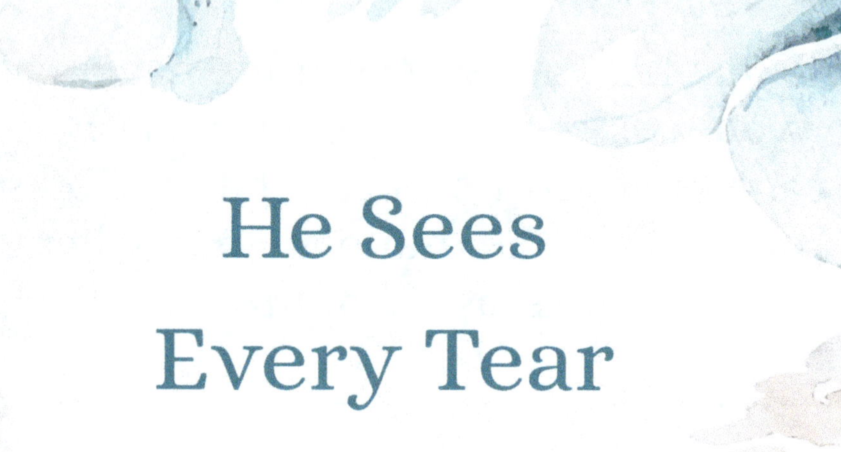

He Sees Every Tear

"You keep track of all my sorrows. You have collected all my tears in your bottle. You have recorded each one in your book."

Psalm 56:8

DEVOTION

Each tear you shed is noted and cherished by God, teaching you that your feelings matter.

REFLECTION

What tearful moments have shaped your journey, and how can you invite God into those sacred spaces?

____

____

____

____

PRAYER

Dear God, thank you for seeing every tear that falls and for holding each moment close to your heart. Help me to remember that I am never alone in my struggles, and guide me to find comfort in your presence.

Every tear you shed is a testament to your strength and a mark of His eternal love.

When You Feel Invisible

"For we are God's masterpiece. He has created us anew in Christ Jesus, so we can do the good things he planned for us long ago."

Ephesians 2:10

DEVOTION

Remember, even in moments when you feel unseen, you are a precious creation with gifts and potential only you can fulfill.

REFLECTION

What moments in your life do you feel unseen or overlooked, and how can you invite God into those feelings today?

____

____

____

____

PRAYER

Dear God, help me to recognize my worth in Your eyes and remind me that I am never truly invisible to You. May Your love fill my heart and grant me peace in the moments when I feel ignored or unnoticed.

In the silent corners of life, His presence whispers, reminding us that we are known and cherished.

When You Feel Overlooked

"Since you are precious and honored in my sight, and because I love you, I will give people in exchange for you, nations in exchange for your life."

Isaiah 43:4

DEVOTION

You are not defined by the recognition of others; your value is inherent and seen by those who truly matter in your life.

REFLECTION

What moments in your life have you felt overlooked, and how can you invite God into those feelings today?

____

____

____

____

PRAYER

Dear Lord, help me to recognize my worth in Your eyes and to remember that I am never unseen by You. Fill my heart with peace as I navigate feelings of being overlooked and remind me of the love you have for me.

Even in the quiet moments, You are writing my story with love and purpose.

You Are Seen and Known

"See what great love the Father has lavished on us, that we should be called children of God! And that is what we are!"

1 John 3:1

DEVOTION

You are cherished beyond measure, and your unique journey is recognized and valued, even in the mundane moments of life.

REFLECTION

What moments in your life have made you feel most deeply seen and understood? How can you invite those feelings into your everyday routines as a reminder of your worth and presence?

____

____

____

____

PRAYER

Dear Lord, remind us today that we are each known and cherished by You. Help us to embrace our identities as loved mothers and women, finding comfort in Your unending grace.

You are seen, you are known, and you are held in the embrace of a love that knows no bounds.

You Are Fully Known and Loved

"You have searched me, Lord, and you know me. You know when I sit and when I rise; you perceive my thoughts from afar. You discern my going out and my lying down; you are familiar with all my ways. Before a word is on my tongue, you, Lord, know it completely."

Psalm 139:1-4

DEVOTION

You are deeply known and loved, both in your beautiful complexity and in the simplicity of being just who you are.

REFLECTION

What does it mean for you to be fully known and loved by God? In what ways do you feel that truth manifest in your life as a mom and a woman today?

____

____

____

____

PRAYER

Dear God, thank you for knowing every part of my heart and life. Help me to embrace your love deeply and to extend that love to those around me.

In your most vulnerable moments, remember that you are cherished beyond measure.

Living Loved

"Beloved, let us love one another, for love is from God; and whoever loves has been born of God and knows God."

1 John 4:7

DEVOTION

Embrace the love that surrounds you, for it empowers you to be the nurturing woman you were created to be.

REFLECTION

What does it mean for you to truly live loved in your daily life, as a mother and a woman? How can you open your heart to embrace the love that surrounds you?

____

____

____

____

PRAYER

Dear Lord, help me to see and embrace the love You have for me in every moment. May I live boldly and freely, filled with the knowledge that I am cherished, just as I am.

Living loved means allowing the warmth of grace to permeate your thoughts and actions.

Your Identity in Christ

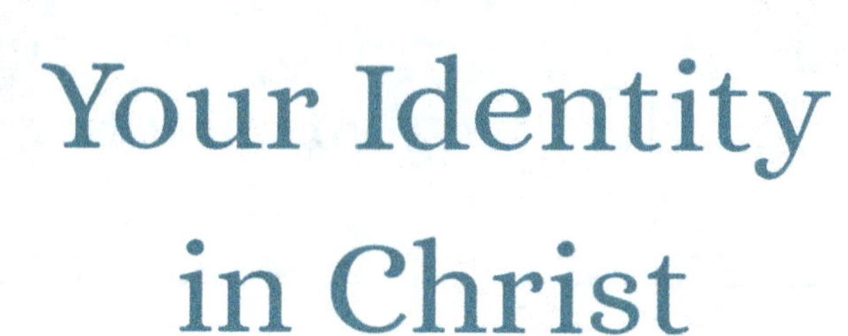

"Therefore, if anyone is in Christ, the new creation has come: The old has gone, the new is here!"

2 Corinthians 5:17

DEVOTION

You are defined by God's love and purpose, not the myriad of roles you fulfill; lean into your true identity in Christ.

REFLECTION

What does being rooted in Christ mean to you, especially during the busy seasons of life? How can you embrace your true identity in Him today?

____

____

____

____

PRAYER

Heavenly Father, thank you for reminding me of who I am in You. Help me to embrace my identity as Your beloved daughter today, filling my heart with confidence and grace.

Your worth is not defined by your to-do list, but by the unchanging love of Christ.

Letting God Define Your Worth

"Delight yourself in the Lord, and He will give you the desires of your heart."

Psalm 37:4

DEVOTION

You are cherished and defined by God's love, not the world's standards.

REFLECTION

What does it look like to let God define your worth in your daily life, especially as a mother and a woman navigating various roles and expectations?

____

____

____

____

PRAYER

Dear God, help me to see myself through Your eyes. Remind me of my intrinsic value in Your love, and guide me to let go of the world's definitions of worth. Amen.

Your worth is not defined by what you do, but by who you are in Christ.

You Are God's Masterpiece

"For we are God's handiwork, created in Christ Jesus to do good works, which God prepared in advance for us to do."

Ephesians 2:10

DEVOTION

You are intricately designed and irreplaceably valued, so embrace the masterpiece you are becoming, knowing that your journey has purpose and beauty just as it is.

REFLECTION

What unique attributes do you possess that reflect God's creativity in your life? How can you honor those traits as part of your journey?

____

____

____

____

PRAYER

Dear Lord, thank You for creating me as Your masterpiece. Help me to see my worth in Your eyes and to embrace the beauty and purpose You have instilled in me.

Your imperfections are part of what makes you uniquely beautiful in the eyes of your Creator.

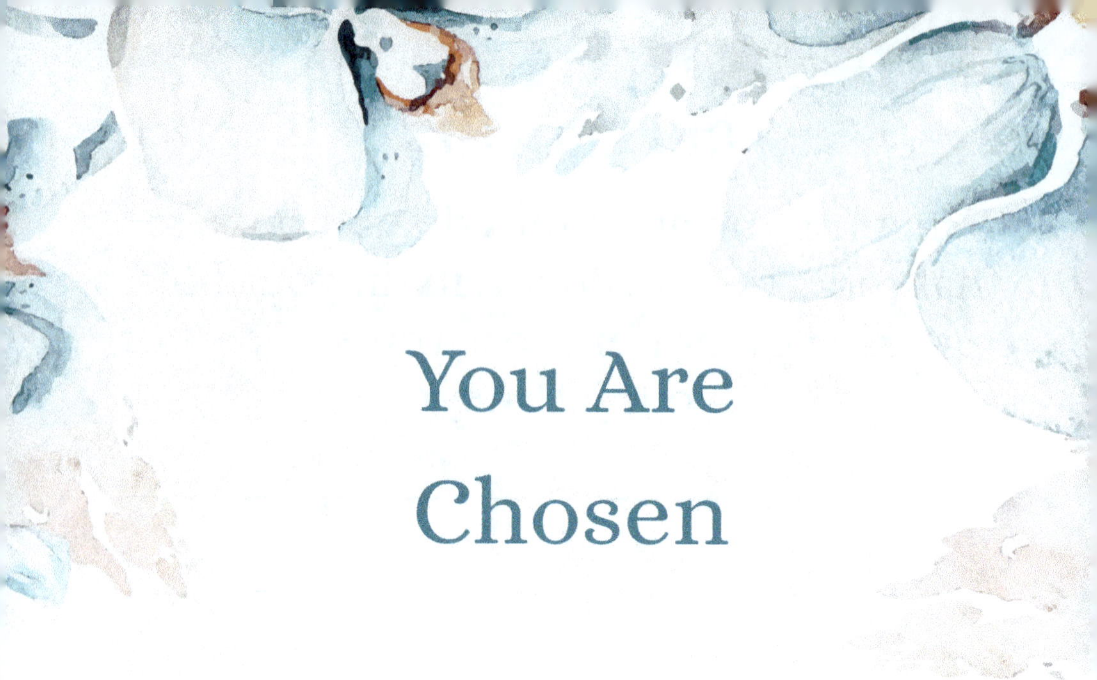

You Are Chosen

"For He chose us in Him before the creation of the world to be holy and blameless in His sight. In love, He predestined us for adoption to sonship through Jesus Christ."

Ephesians 1:4-5

DEVOTION

Remember, dear friend, that you are chosen by a loving God who sees you beyond your roles – you are treasured for who you are, not just what you do.

REFLECTION

What does it mean to you to be chosen by God in your life as a woman and a mother? How does this truth impact the way you see your purpose and your daily routine?

____

____

____

____

PRAYER

Dear God, thank You for choosing me and for the unique path You've laid out before me. Help me to embrace my identity as Your beloved daughter and to walk in the light of that calling each day.

You are not just a passenger in this life; you are the one chosen to steer your ship with grace and courage.

Chosen and Cherished

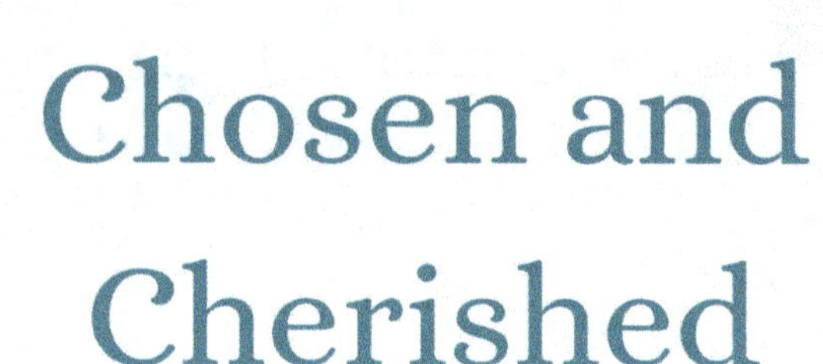

"See, I have engraved you on the palms of my hands; your walls are ever before me."

Isaiah 49:16

DEVOTION

You are chosen for a purpose, and you are cherished not for what you do, but simply for who you are.

REFLECTION

What does it mean for you to feel chosen and cherished in your everyday life, and how can you actively remind yourself of this truth today?

____

____

____

____

PRAYER

Heavenly Father, thank You for reminding us that we are chosen and cherished in Your eyes. Help us to embrace our worth and share that love with those around us. May we find comfort in knowing we are never alone.

You are not just a mother; you are a beloved daughter in the eyes of God.

Halfway Through Our Journey

You are now halfway through this devotional journey.

Many women discover this book through the thoughtful reviews shared by readers like you.

If these pages have supported your faith and daily reflection, would you consider sharing a short review on Amazon?

Your voice may help someone else find encouragement today.

https://devo.anchoredgraces.com/anxiety

He Delights in You

"The Lord your God is with you, the Mighty Warrior who saves. He will take great delight in you; in his love, he will no longer rebuke you, but will rejoice over you with singing."

Zephaniah 3:17

DEVOTION

You are a beloved creation, and your life brings joy to the heart of God.

REFLECTION

What are the ways you can intentionally recognize and embrace the delight that God takes in you, even amidst the chaos of daily life?

____

____

____

____

PRAYER

Dear Lord, thank You for the beautiful truth that You delight in me. Help me to open my heart to receive Your love and to walk each day with the assurance that I am cherished as Your daughter.

Your worth is not measured by your to-do list, but by the love that shapes your heart.

Walking in Confidence, Not Comparison

"Charm is deceptive, and beauty is fleeting; but a woman who fears the Lord is to be praised."

Proverbs 31:30

DEVOTION

Embrace the beauty of your own story and trust that your path is uniquely designed for you, free from the shadows of comparison.

REFLECTION

What areas of your life do you find yourself comparing to others, and how can embracing your unique journey lead to greater peace and confidence today?

____

____

____

____

PRAYER

Dear Lord, help me to see my worth through Your eyes. Let me focus on the gifts and strengths You have given me, and remind me that I am enough just as I am. Grant me the courage to celebrate others without diminishing my own accomplishments.

Your journey is uniquely crafted by God; comparing it to others only blurs the beautiful path meant uniquely for you.

When You Feel Inadequate

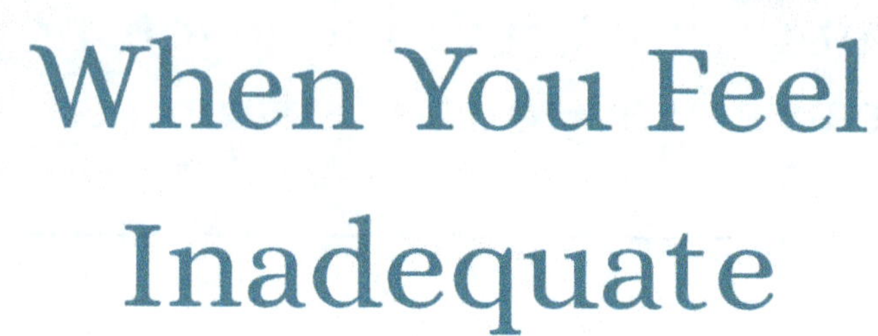

"God is within her, she will not fall; God will help her at break of day."

Psalm 46:5

DEVOTION

You are enough, just as you are, and your genuine love and care are what truly make a difference in your family's life.

REFLECTION

What are the moments in your life when you feel most inadequate, and how can you invite God into those feelings?

____

____

____

____

PRAYER

Dear God, please remind me that in my weakness, you are my strength. Help me embrace my imperfections and find peace in knowing I am enough because of your love.

In the tapestry of life, our imperfections are the threads that make us uniquely beautiful.

Speaking Life Over Yourself

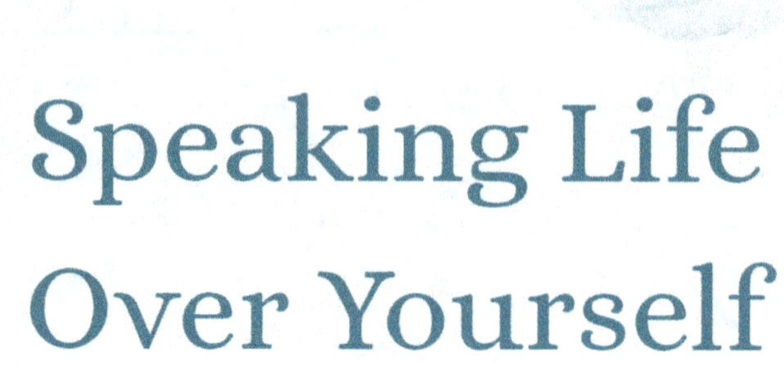

"I praise you because I am fearfully and wonderfully made; your works are wonderful, I know that full well."

Psalm 139:14

DEVOTION

Embrace the truth that your words hold power, and make it a practice to speak life over yourself daily.

REFLECTION

What words do you speak over yourself when you face challenges and uncertainties in your life? How can you shift those words to speak life, affirmation, and grace into your own heart and soul?

____

____

____

____

PRAYER

Dear Lord, help me to see myself through Your loving eyes. May I choose to speak words of hope and encouragement over my life, embracing the beautiful truth of who I am in You.

Your words hold the power to shape your reality; let them reflect the love and strength you carry within.

Living with Holy Confidence

"So do not throw away your confidence; it will be richly rewarded. You need to persevere so that when you have done the will of God, you will receive what He has promised."

Hebrews 10:35-36

DEVOTION

Living with holy confidence means recognizing that your strength is not derived from your circumstances, but from your relationship with God and His promises for your life.

REFLECTION

What does it mean for you to walk confidently in your daily life, embracing your role as a mom and a woman of faith?

____

____

____

____

PRAYER

Dear God, help me to embrace the holy confidence that comes from knowing I am loved and valued by You. Guide my heart and mind as I navigate the joys and challenges of being a woman, and remind me of the strength that lies within Your presence.

Confidence is not perfection; it's the quiet assurance that I am enough, just as I am.

Embracing Grace, Not Perfection

"Consider how the wildflowers grow. They do not labor or spin. Yet I tell you, not even Solomon in all his splendor was dressed like one of these. If that is how God clothes the grass of the field, how much more will he clothe you, you of little faith?"

Luke 12:27-28

DEVOTION

As you embrace your unique journey, remember that grace invites you to let go of perfection and find peace in the beautiful chaos of life.

REFLECTION

What would it look like in your life to embrace grace rather than striving for unattainable perfection? How might your days change if you offered yourself the same kindness and understanding you give to others?

____

____

____

____

PRAYER

Dear God, help me to let go of my need for perfection and to embrace the beautiful messiness of life. Remind me to see Your grace in every moment and to extend it to myself as I navigate the challenges of the present and beyond.

Grace fills the gaps where perfection fails.

Grace That Covers All

"But He said to me, 'My grace is sufficient for you, for my power is made perfect in weakness.' Therefore I will boast all the more gladly of my weaknesses, so that the power of Christ may rest upon me."

2 Corinthians 12:9

DEVOTION

Even in our moments of weakness and uncertainty, God's grace wraps around us, providing reassurance that we are enough just as we are.

REFLECTION

What areas of your life do you need to remind yourself that God's grace covers you completely, despite your imperfections and challenges?

____

____

____

____

PRAYER

Dear God, thank You for Your boundless grace that embraces us even when we feel unworthy. Help us to accept this grace in our lives and extend it to ourselves and others.

Grace is not only a gift; it is the soothing balm that heals our weary souls and reminds us we are loved just as we are.

God's Grace for Past Mistakes

"Therefore, there is now no condemnation for those who are in Christ Jesus."

Romans 8:1

DEVOTION

Your past does not define your worth; God's grace is always available to lift you from the shadows of regret into the light of hope.

REFLECTION

What past mistakes linger in your heart that you need to release to God's grace today? How might embracing His forgiveness change the way you move forward in your life?

____

____

____

____

PRAYER

Dear Lord, thank You for Your endless grace and mercy. Help me to let go of my past and embrace the beauty of new beginnings. Fill my heart with Your peace and guidance as I continue this journey.

God's grace transforms our scars into stories of hope.

Your Past Does Not Define You

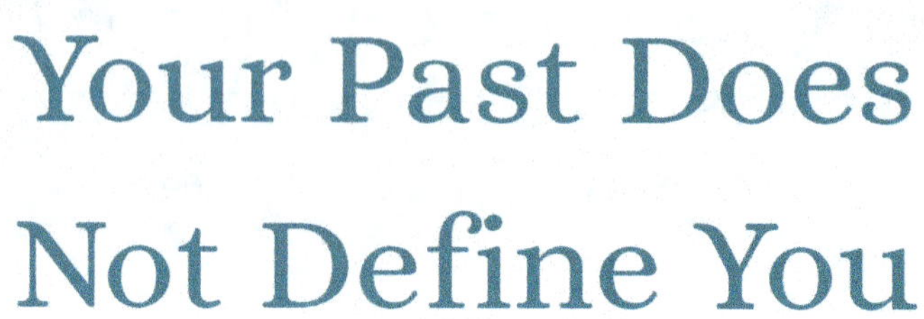

"I praise you because I am fearfully and wonderfully made; your works are wonderful, I know that full well."

Psalm 139:14

DEVOTION

You are not the sum of your past experiences; you are a continually evolving masterpiece, crafted by the hands of love.

REFLECTION

What memories from your past do you find yourself clinging to, and how might you release them to embrace the woman you've become?

____

____

____

____

PRAYER

Dear God, help me to let go of the weight of my past and to see myself through Your loving eyes. Remind me daily that I am defined by Your grace and not by my mistakes.

Your past may shape your story, but it does not have the power to rewrite who you are destined to be.

Letting Go of Shame

"Brothers and sisters, I do not consider myself yet to have taken hold of it. But one thing I do: Forgetting what is behind and straining toward what is ahead, I press on toward the goal to win the prize for which God has called me heavenward in Christ Jesus."

Philippians 3:13-14

DEVOTION

You are not defined by your past, but by the grace that guides you toward a brighter future.

REFLECTION

What are the moments in your life where you've felt shame, and how might letting go of those feelings transform your heart and relationships?

____

____

____

____

PRAYER

Dear God, help me to release the burdens of shame that I have carried. May Your love show me the way to healing and renewal, embracing the truth that I am enough just as I am.

Shame can weigh us down, but grace lifts us up.

Forgiving Yourself and Others

"As far as the east is from the west, so far has he removed our transgressions from us."

Psalm 103:12

DEVOTION

No matter the scars of the past, forgiving ourselves and others opens the door to healing and deeper connections. Remember, as you navigate this journey, both receiving and offering forgiveness is an act of love that nurtures not only your spirit but also the hearts of those around you.

REFLECTION

What are the things you hold onto that keep you from fully embracing compassion for yourself and others? How might letting go of those burdens transform your relationships and inner peace?

____

____

____

____

PRAYER

Dear Lord, help me to extend grace to myself and those I encounter. As I navigate my journey, remind me that forgiveness is a path to healing and restoration.

Forgiveness is not just a gift we give to others; it is the key that unlocks our own heart.

Forgiveness Is Freedom

"Be kind to one another, tenderhearted, forgiving one another, as God in Christ forgave you."

Ephesians 4:32

DEVOTION

Forgiveness is a powerful choice that, when embraced, opens the door to true freedom and an authentic life filled with love and joy.

REFLECTION

What burdens are you holding onto that keep you from experiencing true freedom?

____

____

____

____

PRAYER

Dear God, thank you for the gift of forgiveness. Help me to release the weight of past grievances and embrace the lightness that comes with letting go.

Forgiveness is not just a gift to others; it's a pathway to your own freedom.

Strength to Forgive

"Be kind to one another, tenderhearted, forgiving one another, as God in Christ forgave you."

Ephesians 4:32

DEVOTION

Forgiveness is a gift we give ourselves, freeing our hearts and guiding us toward joy.

REFLECTION

What is one situation in your life where holding onto resentment has weighed you down, and how might choosing forgiveness lighten your heart?

____

____

____

____

PRAYER

Dear God, help me to release the burdens of anger and hurt. Grant me the strength to forgive those who have wronged me, and fill my heart with Your peace.

Forgiveness is not just an act of mercy; it's a gift we give ourselves.

Letting Go
of Bitterness

"See to it that no one falls short of the grace of God and that no bitter root grows up to cause trouble and defile many."

Hebrews 12:15

DEVOTION

Letting go of bitterness is an act of freedom that opens your heart to the joy and love waiting to embrace you.

REFLECTION

What bitterness or unresolved hurt are you carrying that might be weighing you down? How can you begin the process of letting that go today?

____

____

____

____

PRAYER

Dear Lord, help me to release the bitterness in my heart and embrace the freedom that forgiveness brings. Grant me the strength to let go of past hurts and the grace to heal.

Bitterness is like drinking poison and expecting the other person to suffer.

He Restores What Was Broken

Create in me a clean heart, O God, and renew a right spirit within me."

Psalm 51:10

DEVOTION

True restoration begins when we embrace our brokenness and invite God into our hearts, allowing Him to renew our spirits and heal our relationships.

REFLECTION

What areas in your life feel broken or in need of restoration? How can you invite God into those spaces for healing and renewal?

____

____

____

____

PRAYER

Dear Lord, thank You for the promise that You restore what has been broken in our lives. Help me to trust in Your healing power and open my heart to the beautiful transformation You desire for me.

**Out of the ashes,
He brings forth beauty.**

Anchored in His Word

"We have this hope as an anchor for the soul, firm and secure. It enters the inner sanctuary behind the curtain."

Hebrews 6:19

DEVOTION

When the waves of chaos crash around you, remember that God's Word is your steadfast anchor, providing strength and direction for the journey ahead.

REFLECTION

What does it look like in your daily life to be anchored in God's Word, especially when faced with challenges as a mom?

____

____

____

____

PRAYER

Dear God, thank You for Your unwavering presence in our lives. Help me to find solace and strength in Your Word each day, guiding me to be a light for my family and those around me.

When we are anchored in His Word, our souls find peace amidst life's storms.

The Anchor of God's Word

"For we live by faith, not by sight."

2 Corinthians 5:7

DEVOTION

The storms of life may be fierce, yet a steadfast reliance on God's Word provides the focus and strength we need to navigate through any challenge.

REFLECTION

What verses or promises from God's Word have anchored you during challenging seasons in your life? How can you intentionally hold onto those truths today?

____

____

____

____

PRAYER

Dear Lord, thank you for the gift of Your Word, a steadfast anchor in our lives. Help us to lean into its wisdom and find solace as we navigate each day with grace and clarity.

In times of storm, His promises become our safe harbor.

The Power of God's Word

"For the word of God is alive and active. Sharper than any double-edged sword, it penetrates even to dividing soul and spirit, joints and marrow; it judges the thoughts and attitudes of the heart."

Hebrews 4:12

DEVOTION

The ability to nourish our spirits through God's Word allows us to approach life's challenges with renewed perspective and strength.

REFLECTION

What words are you holding on to today that speak life into your circumstances, and how can you lean more into God's promises to guide you?

____

____

____

____

PRAYER

Dear Heavenly Father, thank You for the gift of Your Word, a beacon of truth in our lives. Help me to lean on its promises and find strength in its wisdom as I navigate my days.

God's Word is a balm for the weary soul, offering peace and clarity amidst life's storms.

Becoming a Woman of the Word

"Your word is a lamp for my feet, a light on my path."

Psalm 119:105

DEVOTION

Let the Word of God be your guide and source of strength, reminding you that it's not just about being a parent or a professional; it's about nurturing your spirit and wisdom for all the roles you carry.

REFLECTION

What are the ways you can immerse yourself in God's Word this week, and how can it shape your thoughts and actions as a mother and woman of faith?

____

____

____

____

PRAYER

Dear Lord, thank you for the gift of Your Word. Help me to dive deeper into its truths and allow those truths to envelop my heart and guide my life. Amen.

Becoming a woman of the Word is not just about reading; it's about living the love and wisdom found on its pages.

Finding Comfort in Scripture

"The Lord is close to the brokenhearted and saves those who are crushed in spirit."

Psalm 34:18

DEVOTION

In moments of struggle, remember that God's love surrounds you and His comfort awaits.

REFLECTION

What scripture has brought you comfort in challenging times, and how can you remind yourself of its truth today?

____

____

____

____

PRAYER

Dear God, thank you for your loving presence in my life. Help me to open my heart to your word and find solace in the promises you offer through scripture.

Your soul finds rest in the pages of His Word.

Healing Through Scripture

"Bless the Lord, O my soul, and forget not all his benefits, who forgives all your iniquity, who heals all your diseases."

Psalm 103:2-3

DEVOTION

In moments of weariness, revisit the scriptures, for within them lies the healing balm your spirit longs for.

REFLECTION

What is a scripture that brings you peace or comfort during difficult times, and how can you lean into that verse this week as you seek healing?

____

____

____

____

PRAYER

Dear Lord, as I turn to Your Word, help me to find solace and strength in your promises. May Your healing touch renew my spirit and fill my heart with hope and joy.

Scripture is not just words on a page; it is the balm that soothes the soul and ignites the spirit.

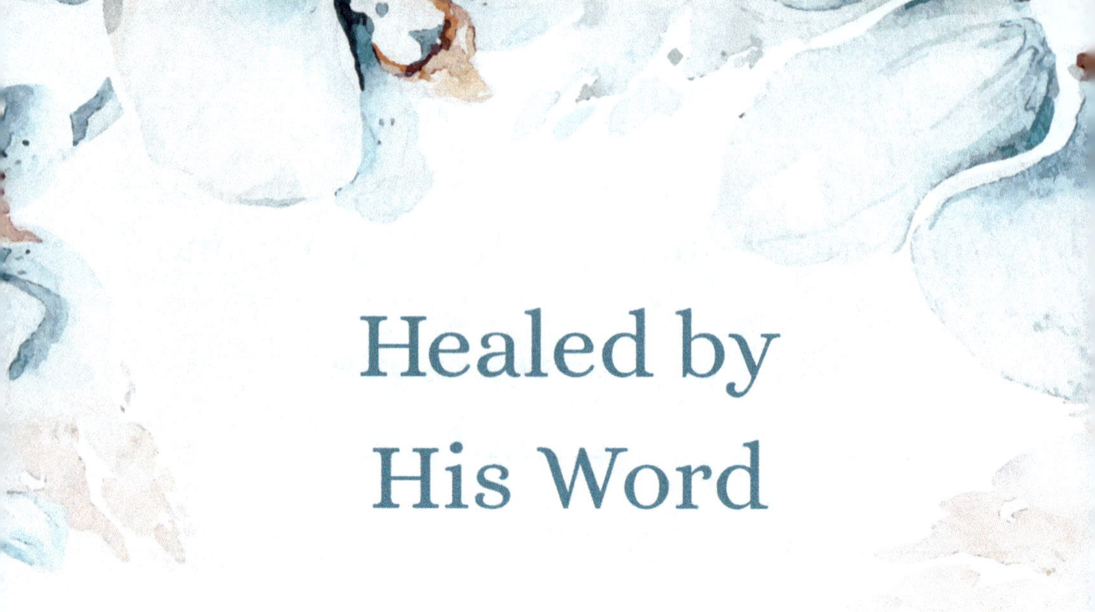

Healed by His Word

James 1:21 tells us to "humbly accept the word planted in you, which can save you."

DEVOTION

The healing power of His Word is always within reach; we simply need to pause and listen.

REFLECTION

What is one negative thought or belief about yourself that God's Word can help you replace with truth?

____

____

____

____

PRAYER

Dear Lord, thank You for Your Word, which has the power to heal and transform our hearts. Help me to embrace Your promises and find comfort in Your truth today.

Healing begins when we allow His voice to drown out our doubts.

Rooted in God's Truth

"But whose delight is in the law of the Lord, and who meditates on His law day and night. That person is like a tree planted by streams of water, which yields its fruit in season and whose leaf does not wither—whatever they do prospers."

Psalm 1:2-3

DEVOTION

Being rooted in God's truth provides stability and nourishment amidst the chaos of daily life, reminding you that you are never alone in your journey.

REFLECTION

What does it mean for you to be truly rooted in God's truth amidst the busyness of daily life?

____

____

____

____

PRAYER

Dear God, thank You for the foundation of Your truth in my life. Help me to stay grounded in Your Word and to reflect Your love and wisdom to those around me.

Rooted in God's truth, we can weather any storm and nourish the seeds of love and hope in our families.

Guarding Your Heart

"Above all else, guard your heart, for everything you do flows from it."

Proverbs 4:23

DEVOTION

The heart is a precious treasure; guard it with intention, nurturing what brings you joy and releasing what holds you back.

REFLECTION

What are the specific areas of your life where you need to be more intentional about guarding your heart against negativity or hurtful influences?

____

____

____

____

PRAYER

Dear Lord, help me to guard my heart with wisdom and grace. May I find strength in Your love, shielding me from hurt and negativity as I navigate my role as a mom, friend, and woman of faith.

Your heart is a precious treasure; guard it well to nurture the love it holds.

Decluttering the Soul

"Create in me a clean heart, O God, and renew a right spirit within me."

Psalm 51:10

DEVOTION

Sometimes, decluttering our physical space can lead to profound emotional and spiritual renewal, reminding us that it's alright to let go of the old to make way for the new.

REFLECTION

What old thoughts or emotional burdens are you holding onto that no longer serve your spirit?

____

____

____

____

PRAYER

Dear Lord, help me to recognize what's cluttering my heart and mind. Cleanse my spirit and guide me as I let go of the unnecessary, making space for Your love and peace.

Just as a physical space can become cluttered, so too can our souls; it's time to clear out what no longer nurtures us.

A Moment of Gratitude

If this devotional has brought moments of peace, strength, or reflection into your life, a short review on Amazon can help others discover it too.

https://devo.anchoredgraces.com/anxiety

Even a few words about your experience can make a meaningful difference.

Thank you for continuing this journey.

Choosing Rest Over Rush

"Come to me, all you who are weary and burdened, and I will give you rest."

Luke 11:28.

DEVOTION

In the midst of the whirlwind of daily responsibilities, remember that taking time to rest is not about neglecting duties but embracing the sacred act of self-care, allowing ourselves to recharge and be present for those we love.

REFLECTION

What in your life feels rushed right now, and how can you intentionally create space for rest amidst the demands of life and daily responsibilities?

____

____

____

____

PRAYER

Dear God, please help me embrace moments of stillness in the chaos of my life. Teach me to prioritize rest and to find Your peace in the midst of my busyness. Amen.

Rest is not the absence of work; it's the presence of peace.

Rest for the Weary

Matthew 6:31-33 reminds us not to worry about our needs but to seek first the kingdom of God and His righteousness. As we shift our focus, we find that His provision meets us in the most unexpected ways, often when we feel we have nothing left to give.

DEVOTION

In moments of weariness, remember that your worth is not tied to your productivity, but to the love and grace you give freely.

REFLECTION

What do you do to find rest amidst the busyness of your life, and how can you intentionally carve out moments of peace for yourself today?

____

____

____

____

PRAYER

Dear God, thank You for being a refuge for our weary hearts. Please help me to embrace the rest You offer and to prioritize moments of stillness in my hectic schedule.

Rest is not merely the absence of work; it is the presence of peace.

Restoring Your Soul

"He refreshes my soul. He guides me along the right paths for His name's sake."

Psalm 23:3

DEVOTION

Sometimes, the most profound moments of renewal come from simply carving out intentional time to breathe and reflect, allowing your soul to regain its strength.

REFLECTION

What does your soul long for in this season of your life, and how can you create space to nurture that need each day?

____

____

____

____

PRAYER

Dear God, help me embrace the quiet moments where my soul can find rest. Restore in me a sense of peace and joy that rejuvenates my spirit and nourishes my heart. Amen.

In the stillness, your soul whispers what it truly needs.

Resting in God's Rhythm

"Come to me, all you who are weary and burdened, and I will give you rest. Take my yoke upon you and learn from me, for I am gentle and humble in heart, and you will find rest for your souls. For my yoke is easy and my burden is light."

Matthew 11:28-30

DEVOTION

In the whirlwind of life, remember that resting in God's rhythm means allowing Him to shoulder your burdens while you nurture your spirit.

REFLECTION

What does it look like for you to truly rest in God's rhythm during your busy days as a mom?

____

____

____

____

PRAYER

Lord, help me to quiet my heart and mind, recognizing the beauty of resting in Your presence. Teach me to embrace Your rhythm and find peace in each moment.

Resting in God's rhythm allows us to find joy in each day's unfolding.

Abiding in the Vine

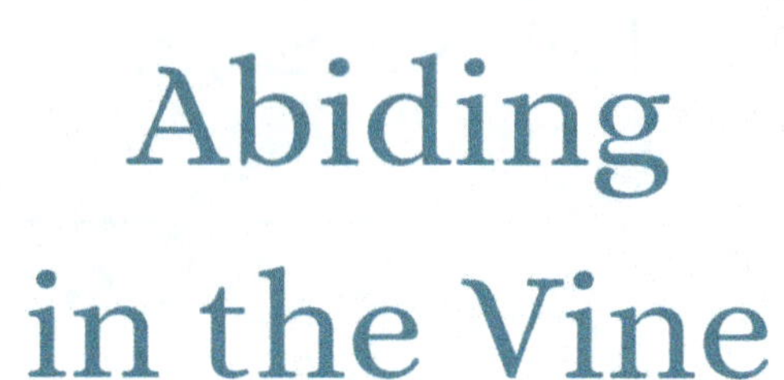

"I am the vine; you are the branches. If you remain in me and I in you, you will bear much fruit; apart from me, you can do nothing."

John 15:5

DEVOTION

In this season of life, remember that true strength and fruitfulness flow from your relationship with God; prioritize abiding in Him, and He will guide you through the busyness with grace and clarity.

REFLECTION

What does it mean for you to truly abide in Jesus amidst your daily responsibilities as a mother and friend?

____

____

____

____

PRAYER

Dear God, thank You for being the true Vine in our lives. Help me to stay connected to You, drawing strength, love, and wisdom as I navigate my daily walk. May I find peace and joy in Your presence today.

Abiding in the Vine means finding strength in His love, especially when life feels overwhelming.

Abiding in Peace

"Abide in me, and I in you. As the branch cannot bear fruit by itself, unless it abides in the vine, neither can you, unless you abide in me."

John 15:4

DEVOTION

In the rush of life, it can be easy to sideline our need for peace, believing we can handle everything on our own. However, true peace comes from remaining rooted in faith and allowing God's grace to flow through us, even amidst the busyness of everyday life and work.

REFLECTION

What does it look like for you to truly abide in peace amidst the busyness of womhood and daily life?

____

____

____

____

PRAYER

Dear God, as I navigate the challenges of each day, help me to find your peace in every moment. Remind me that I can rest in you, letting go of worries and embracing your love. Thank you for your gentle presence.

Peace is not the absence of trouble, but the presence of Christ.

Rooted and Grounded in Love

Ephesians 3:17-19 reminds us of the profound depth of God's love that binds us together: "that Christ may dwell in your hearts through faith, and that you, being rooted and grounded in love, may have strength to comprehend with all the saints what is the breadth and length and height and depth of love."

DEVOTION

Remember that when you root yourself in the nourishing love of God, you grow in strength and grace, allowing you to share that love abundantly with those around you.

REFLECTION

What does it mean for you to feel rooted and grounded in love amidst the busyness of daily life? How can you cultivate that sense of stability and connection in your relationships?

____

____

____

____

PRAYER

Dear God, thank You for the gift of love that surrounds me. Help me to root myself deeper in Your love so I can reflect that same love to my family and others around me. Amen.

Love is not just a sentiment; it's the foundation that holds us steady in the storms of life.

Rooted in God's Love

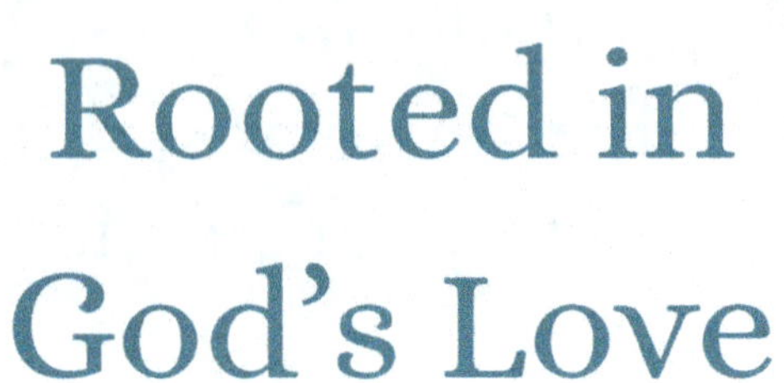

"But the love of the Lord remains forever with those who fear him. His salvation extends to the children's children."

Psalm 103:17

DEVOTION

In every season of womanhood, remember that your worth is rooted in God's unchanging love, not in your accomplishments or challenges.

REFLECTION

What does it mean for you to feel truly rooted in God's love amidst the daily challenges of life? How can you identify and nurture that love in your day-to-day experiences?

____

____

____

____

PRAYER

Dear God, thank you for surrounding me with your love and grace. Help me to anchor my heart in you, so that I may share that love with my family and those around me.

Rooted in God's love, we thrive even in the stormy seasons of life.

The Gift of His Presence

"The Lord is near to all who call on Him,
to all who call on Him in truth."

Psalm 145:18

DEVOTION

Embrace the quiet moments, for they
are often where you can feel His
presence the strongest.

REFLECTION

What does it mean to you, in the midst of your busy life as a mom, to intentionally seek the presence of God each day?

____

____

____

____

PRAYER

Heavenly Father, thank You for the gift of Your presence in our lives. Help us to slow down and be aware of You around us, finding comfort and strength in Your love today.

In the stillness, we find Him waiting, ready to embrace us with peace.

Refreshed by His Presence

"You make known to me the path of life;
in your presence there is fullness of joy;
at your right hand are pleasures
forevermore."

Psalm 16:11

DEVOTION

In the rush of life's demands, taking
time to encounter God can renew our
spirits and remind us of our true joy.

REFLECTION

What moments in your day can you intentionally set aside to encounter God's presence and be refreshed by His love?

____

____

____

____

PRAYER

Dear Lord, thank you for your constant presence in our lives. Help us to seek you amid the busyness, finding peace and joy in the time we spend with you.

In the quiet moments, His presence is a gentle reminder of who we truly are.

The Power of Prayer

Philippians 4:6-7 reminds us not to be anxious, but to bring everything to God in prayer. In a world filled with responsibilities, uncertainties, and the beautiful chaos of life, prayer can be our quiet refuge and strength.

DEVOTION

In the midst of life's busyness, remember that prayer is not just a ritual but a lifeline that connects you to divine guidance and peace.

REFLECTION

What are the prayers you whisper in the quiet moments of your day, and how do you feel God's presence within those sacred exchanges?

____

____

____

____

PRAYER

Dear Lord, thank you for the gift of prayer, a lifeline to connect with You amid life's busyness. Help me to remember that in every moment of chaos, I can find peace in Your presence.

Prayer is not just about asking; it's about listening to the whisper of God in your heart.

Becoming a Prayerful Woman

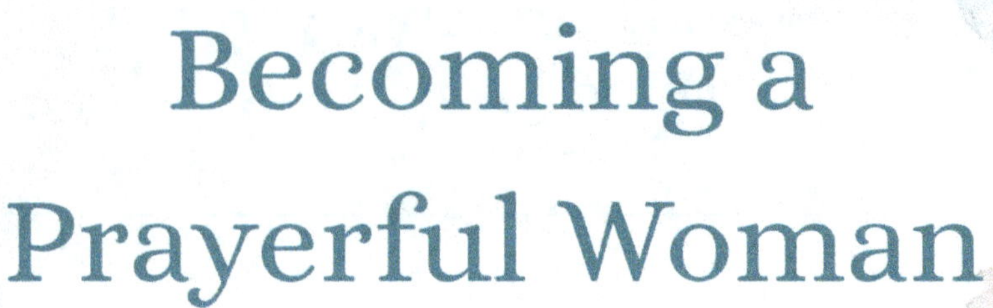

"Pray without ceasing."

1 Thessalonians 5:17

DEVOTION

In cultivating a prayerful heart, we learn that even the simplest conversations with God can nourish our souls and ground us in His presence.

REFLECTION

What does a prayerful life look like for you, and how can you nurture that relationship with God in your busy days?

____

____

____

____

PRAYER

Dear Lord, as I navigate the complexities of life, remind me to turn to You in prayer. Help me cultivate a heart that seeks You first and finds peace in Your presence.

Prayer is not just asking; it is listening for the whisper of God in the midst of our busy lives.

Persevering in Prayer

"Rejoice in hope, be patient in tribulation, be constant in prayer."

Romans 12:12

DEVOTION

In the midst of life's storms, remember that your perseverance in prayer strengthens your spirit and shapes your journey.

REFLECTION

What areas in your life feel heavy or unyielding right now, and how can you invite God into those moments through prayer?

____

____

____

____

PRAYER

Dear God, thank you for always being present in our lives. Help me to trust in Your timing and to keep my heart open as I persevere in prayer, knowing You hear me.

Persistent prayer cultivates patience and opens doors we couldn't imagine.

Your Prayers Matter

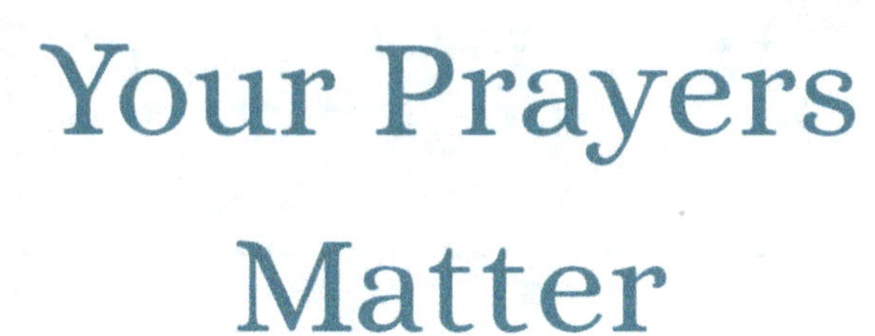

"Call to me and I will answer you and tell you great and unsearchable things you do not know."

Jeremiah 33:3

DEVOTION

Your prayers, however simple or desperate, are powerful tools that shape not just your life but the lives of those you love.

REFLECTION

What worries or hopes have you been holding in your heart lately? How can you invite God into those moments through prayer?

____

____

____

____

PRAYER

Dear Lord, thank you for listening to my heart and for the assurance that my prayers matter. Help me to lean into Your presence and trust in Your perfect timing.

Every whispered prayer is a seed planted in faith, waiting for God's garden to bloom.

Trusting God's Timing

"Trust in the Lord with all your heart and lean not on your own understanding."

Proverbs 3:5-6

DEVOTION

In this season of your life, remember that every moment is an opportunity to deepen your trust in God's plan; His timing will lead you to places you never thought you'd go.

REFLECTION

What areas of your life do you find yourself struggling to trust God's timing? How might surrendering these concerns to Him change your perspective?

____

____

____

____

PRAYER

Dear Lord, help me to embrace your perfect timing in my life. Remind me that your plans for me are good, allowing me to find peace and trust in each moment.

Patience is not just waiting; it's a chance to grow in grace.

Near the End of Our Journey

You have spent many days reflecting through these devotionals.

If this book has supported your spiritual journey, sharing a short review on Amazon helps more women discover these pages of encouragement.

https://devo.anchoredgraces.com/anxiety

Your story may be the reason another woman finds hope.

God's Perfect Timing

"And we know that in all things God works for the good of those who love him, who have been called according to his purpose."

Romans 8:28

DEVOTION

Trust that the moments you feel most uncertain are often the moments that God is preparing you for something extraordinary.

REFLECTION

What areas of your life are you struggling to understand God's timing? How might surrendering those feelings open your heart to His plans?

____

____

____

____

PRAYER

Dear Lord, thank You for always knowing what is best for us. Help me to trust Your perfect timing in my life, even when I can't see the path ahead.

Trusting in God's perfect timing allows us to find peace in every season.

Waiting Well with God

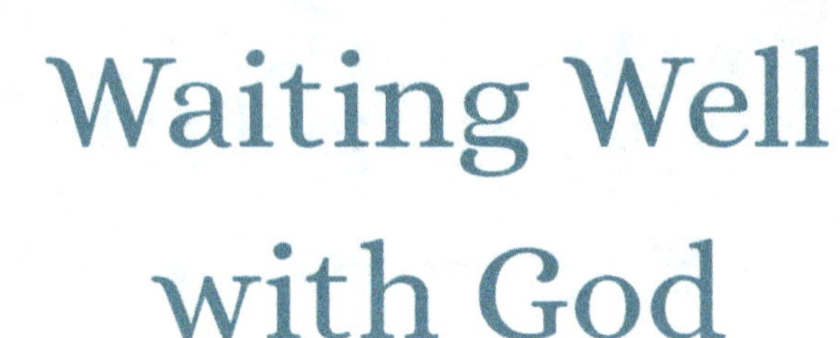

"Wait for the Lord; be strong and take heart and wait for the Lord."

Psalm 27:14

DEVOTION

God invites us to experience His presence even in our waiting, teaching us that the journey can be just as profound as the destination.

REFLECTION

What does waiting on God look like for you in this season of your life, and how can you embrace that waiting with hope and trust?

____

____

____

____

PRAYER

Dear God, thank you for being with me in every season. Help me to find joy and purpose as I wait on You, trusting that Your timing is perfect.

Waiting is not a time of inactivity, but an opportunity to deepen our relationship with God.

God's Presence in the Waiting

"I waited patiently for the Lord; he turned to me and heard my cry. He lifted me out of the slimy pit, out of the mud and mire; he set my feet on a rock and gave me a firm place to stand. He put a new song in my mouth, a hymn of praise to our God."

Psalm 40:1-3

DEVOTION

In the seasons of waiting, trust that you are never alone; God's presence is there, guiding you toward His perfect plan.

REFLECTION

What areas of your life feel like they're on pause right now, and how can you invite God to be present with you in that waiting?

____

____

____

____

PRAYER

Dear God, thank You for being with us in every season of our lives, especially during the moments of waiting. Help us to feel Your comforting presence as we navigate this journey, trusting that You are at work in ways we may not yet see.

God's silence does not mean He is absent; it often means He is preparing us for something more beautiful.

Faith in the Storm

"Now faith is confidence in what we hope for and assurance about what we do not see."

Hebrews 11:1

DEVOTION

When the storms of life rage, remember that your faith is not only your refuge but also a powerful force that can guide you through the toughest times.

REFLECTION

What storms are you currently facing in your life, and how can you invite God into those turbulent moments for comfort and guidance?

____

____

____

____

PRAYER

Dear God, in the midst of life's storms, help me to trust in Your presence. Calm my heart and fill me with hope as I navigate through the waves that threaten to overwhelm me.

Faith doesn't eliminate the storm; it assures us of the anchor we have in the midst of it.

Strength for the Journey

"She is clothed with strength and dignity;
she can laugh at the days to come."

Proverbs 31:25

DEVOTION

Strength for our journey often comes
from acknowledging both our struggles
and our joys, making us resilient and
beautifully imperfect.

REFLECTION

What are the challenges you're currently facing, and how can you invite God's strength into your journey today?

____

____

____

____

PRAYER

Dear God, thank You for being our source of strength. As I navigate the challenges of womanhood and life, fill me with Your peace and guide my steps with Your unwavering support.

Your strength is not just about enduring; it's about embracing the journey with grace and hope.

Thank you for spending this devotional journey with Anchored Grace.

If this devotional encouraged your heart, strengthened your faith, or brought peace to your daily routine, would you consider leaving a short review on Amazon?

https://devo.anchoredgraces.com/anxiety

Reviews help other women discover devotionals that may support them through their own seasons of life.

Even a single sentence about your experience can make a difference.

We are grateful you chose Anchored Grace.